# COUNTRIES IN OUR WORLD

SPAIN

*Sean Ryan*

# W
# FRANKLIN WATTS
## LONDON•SYDNEY

This edition published in 2012 by
**Franklin Watts**
338 Euston Road
London NW1 3BH

Franklin Watts Australia
Level 17/207 Kent Street
Sydney NSW 2000

Produced for Franklin Watts by
White-Thomson Publishing Ltd

+44 (0) 845 362 8240
www.wtpub.co.uk

**Series consultant:** Rob Bowden
**Editor:** Sonya Newland
**Designer:** Alix Wood
**Picture researcher:** Amy Sparks

A CIP catalogue record for this book is available from
the British Library.

ISBN 978 1 4451 0811 7

Dewey Classification: 914.6

**Picture Credits**
**Corbis:** Cover (David Samuel Robbins), 9 (O.
Alamany & E. Vicens), 14 (Chris Sattleberger),
15 (Paul Hanna/Reuters), 18 (Daiju Kitamura/AFLO
SPORT/Icon SMI), 20 (Charles O'Rear), 21 (Albert
Gea/Reuters), 24 (Manual H. de Leon/epa), 26
(Laurent Dard/Reuters); **Dreamstime:** 4 (Joe Stark),
7 (Faberfoto), 8 (Haak78), 12 (Jarnogz), 25 (Gvictoria),
29 (Jarnogz); **iStock:** 10 (Elena Aliaga), 28 (Graham
Heywood); **Fotolia:** 11 (Marta P), 22 (Freefly);
**Photoshot:** 27 (EFE/UPPA); **Shutterstock:** 1 (Regien
Paassen), 6 (PixAchi), 17 (Geanina Bechea), 23
(Regien Paassen); **Simon Rice:** 13, 16, 19.

Printed in Malaysia

Franklin Watts is a division of Hachette
Children's Books, an Hachette UK company.
www.hachette.co.uk

# Contents

Introducing Spain     4

Landscapes and environment     8

Population and migration     12

Culture and lifestyles     16

Economy and trade     20

Government and politics     24

Spain in 2020     28

Glossary     30

Further information     31

Index     32

# Introducing Spain

*Spain is situated on the Iberian Peninsula, at the far western end of Europe. In the last 50 years, Spain has changed from being one of the most isolated countries in the Western world to having global connections. It is now an important and influential country as part of the European Union, and Spanish is the third most common language in the world, after Chinese Mandarin and English.*

▲ *Spain has three international borders, a short border with Gibraltar, a British territory, and includes the Canary Islands.*

## The heart of Spain

Spain is divided into several regions, each with different landscapes and peoples. Castile, in the middle of the country, is centred around the capital, Madrid, and has a harsh landscape of broad plains and rugged mountains. The name Castile means 'Land of Castles', and there are many forts on the hilltops of Castile. The people who live there – Castilians – have been the dominant force in Spain since the fifteenth century. They sponsored the first voyages of discovery to the Americas and established colonies there, making Spain the world's first major colonial power.

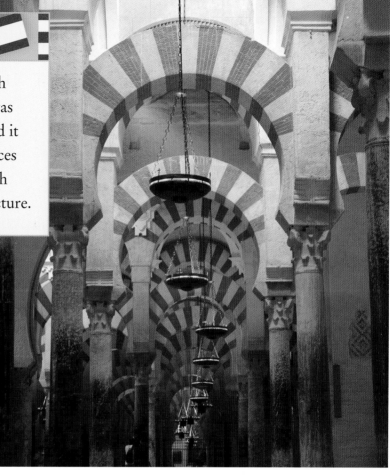

## IT'S A FACT!

When it was built during the eighth century, the mosque at Cordoba was the second largest in the world, and it was one of the most important places in the Islamic Empire. The Moorish influence can be seen in its architecture.

▶ *The inside of the mosque at Cordoba has more than 1,000 pillars supporting arches designed in the Moorish style. It became a Roman Catholic cathedral in 1236 CE.*

## Moorish influences

Castile was formed in the eighth century, when a number of smaller kingdoms joined together to fight a group of Islamic peoples from North Africa called the Moors, who were invading the Iberian Peninsula. The Moors conquered much of Spain, and the area they ruled was called Al-Andaluz. The modern region Andalusia covers most of southern Spain and the Moorish influence is still strong there – it can be seen in the architecture and food, for example. This is the most populated of Spain's regions, and the people who live here are called Andalusians.

## The Mediterranean

Along the coast of the Mediterranean Sea – Spain's top tourist destination – is a region called Catalonia. The Catalans were a great seafaring and trading nation long before the Castilians set off to explore foreign lands. Influences from the time when Spain was part of the Roman Empire can still be seen in Catalonia, particularly in the language, Catalan, which is closely related to Latin. The capital, Barcelona, is considered one of the world's greatest cultural centres today.

▲ *The Guggenheim Museum is one of the most famous landmarks in Bilbao, in the Basque Country. It houses work by both Spanish and international artists.*

## An inward view

The Basque Country crosses the border into France. Cut off by mountains and the sea, the Basques are an ancient people who speak Euskara, a language that is not related to any other. Many of the world's pioneering navigators were Basque people, and Basque vessels were renowned for being the best in the world. The Basques adapted this heritage during the Industrial Revolution, and today the region is still Spain's industrial heartland, based around the great port city of Bilbao.

## The far west

The far western region of Galicia, jutting into the Atlantic Ocean, has been isolated from the rest of the country for much of Spain's history. The people who live there have Celtic origins, and still have much in common with the Irish and the Scots. Galicia has its own language, Gallego, which is a Romance language of Latin origin, like Spanish and Catalan. Galicia has been nicknamed 'the land of a thousand rivers', because so many rivers and streams run through it.

## BASIC DATA

**Official Name:** **Kingdom of Spain**

**Capital:** **Madrid**

**Size:** **504,782 sq km (194,897 sq miles)**

**Population:** **47,042,984**

**Currency:** **Euro**

## Spain today

Throughout history, Spain's fortunes have risen and fallen. It has conquered many areas but has also been torn apart by civil wars. It has been one of the world's greatest powers and one of Europe's poorest countries. Rivalries between the different regions affect its politics, and its varied geography plays an important part in the economy. But Spain's ties to the Mediterranean and Islamic worlds, and the legacy of its empire in Latin America, make it a unique 'bridge' between these regions and its place in Europe.

## FAMOUS SPANIARD

### Francisco Franco
### (1892–1975)

Francisco Franco ruled Spain from the end of the Spanish Civil War in 1939 until 1975. He was the only fascist dictator to remain in power after World War II (1939-45). It is believed that more than 130,000 people were murdered on Franco's orders during this time.

▼ *People enjoy boating in a park in Madrid, which became Spain's capital in 1561.*

*Spain has an extremely varied landscape. The mainland is noted for its high mountain ranges, called sierras, including the Pyrenees, which form a natural boundary between Spain and its neighbour, France. The Balearic Islands in the Mediterranean Sea and the sub-tropical Canary Islands in the Atlantic Ocean, off the coast of North Africa, add to the diversity of Spain's landscapes and environments.*

**PLACE IN THE WORLD**

Total area: **504,782 sq km (194,897 sq miles)**

Percentage of world land area: **0.34%**

World ranking: **51st**

## Warm weather

The rugged north coast of Spain faces the stormy Atlantic Ocean. A high mountain range, called the Cordillera Cantabrica, closely follows the coast, where warm, moist air produces a lot of rainfall. The coastline along the south-east of the country has its own Mediterranean climate, with hot summers and mild winters. However, most of the mainland is a high, dry plateau called the Meseta Central. This has a continental climate, with severe cold in winter and extreme heat in summer.

▼ *Spain's highest mountain, El Teide on the Canary Island of Tenerife, is a dormant volcano in one of the country's 14 national parks.*

## Europe's last wilderness

Much of the Meseta is dry scrubland called *dehesa*. There are some desert areas, but this huge region is divided by the sierras. The high mountain peaks cause rainfall that feeds the rivers, including Spain's largest river, the Ebro. The mountains and river valleys provide shelter for dense forests to grow – nearly 30 per cent of Spain is covered in forest, more compared to the country's land area than many other European countries. Few people live in the forest areas, and some species of animal, especially large mammals such as wolves and bears, have survived here when they have become extinct in much of the rest of Europe. The Canary Islands are also known worldwide for their wildlife, and four of Spain's 14 national parks can be found there.

▲ *Bears are being reintroduced to the Pyrenees from forests in Eastern Europe as part of a joint venture between Spain and France.*

### IT'S A FACT!

After the last breeding female bear in the Pyrenees was killed by a French hunter in 2004, the French and Spanish governments stepped up a programme of bringing more bears from Slovenia in Eastern Europe to be released into the mountains. Today, the bear population is on the rise.

## Spain's threatened landscape

As in many countries, some of Spain's natural environments are under threat. Forests have been destroyed by fires, but others are being cut down to make way for building developments as the country's population increases and more space is needed for human settlement. Global climate change threatens much of the Meseta with desertification. Spain receives a lot of rainfall, but there are still water shortages, as more and more water from the rivers is used for irrigating farmland. Wetland areas are also shrinking as water is diverted from rivers, and this is threatening the wildlife that make the wetlands their home.

> ### IT'S A FACT!
>
> Spain is a very important location for bird migration between Africa and Europe because it is one of only three routes across the Mediterranean. The others are Libya to the toe of Italy and the coastal regions of the eastern Mediterranean.

▼ *The wetlands around Spanish deltas – where rivers enter the sea – are important habitats for wildlife, but water shortages are now threatening these areas.*

▲ *Spain is a world leader in solar power. Solar farms use huge panels like these to capture the energy from sunlight and turn it into electricity.*

## A sustainable future

Spain is a world leader in using renewable energy sources – such as the sun, wind and water – to generate electricity. Spain's thousands of rivers are used to generate hydroelectricity as well as for irrigation. Spain is also Europe's second biggest producer of electricity from wind power, after Germany, but because Spain has only half the population of Germany, this makes its environmental record more impressive. The Navarre region of Spain has a programme that is working towards supplying all the region's energy needs from renewable resources.

### GLOBAL LEADER

**Solar power**

In 2008, the largest solar farm in the world opened in south-east Spain. The Jumilla farm is made up of 120,000 solar panels that convert sunlight into electricity, which can power 20,000 homes. Using renewable resources like the sun helps preserve supplies of fossil fuels, which are running out, and reduces the amount of carbon dioxide being released into the atmosphere.

The people who live in Spain's different regions have their own cultures and traditions, but Spain has also become a multicultural society thanks to the large number of immigrants that have settled there, particularly in the last 20 years.

**PLACE IN THE WORLD**

Population: **47,042,984**

Percentage of world total: **0.67%**

World ranking: **27th**

## Migration to the cities

In the middle of the nineteenth century, people began moving from the countryside in the west and south of Spain, to the cities that were growing up in the north-east in places such as the Basque Country and Catalonia. They hoped to find better job opportunities there, and to improve their quality of life. This resulted in the spread of traditions from one part of the country to another, as the migrants kept alive their own cultures by celebrating traditional customs and fiestas.

▶ *This 'whale parade' is part of the traditional Semana Grande fiesta in the Basque Country.*

## Fleeing abroad

During and after the Spanish Civil War (1936), many refugees from the Basque Country and Catalonia crossed the Pyrenees to France, because they were afraid of staying in Spain while it was ruled by Francisco Franco. Refugees from Galicia and Asturias in the north-west emigrated across the Atlantic Ocean and settled in the USA. Later, even more Spanish people from all regions moved to wealthy countries, especially Germany, in search of better prospects. Emigration caused problems for Spain in the second half of the twentieth century. The economy declined because so many people moved abroad. This especially affected rural areas, where there were not enough young people to work on the farms or enough children to keep schools open.

## Immigration

During the 1970s, Spain's fortunes began to rise, and when Franco died many migrants returned home. In 1986, Spain joined the European Union (EU). This meant that its links with other European countries were strengthened, and the economy began to improve. People from other countries started moving to Spain and immigrants now make up about 10 per cent of the population – far more than in any other EU country. Spain's long history of migration and emigration means that most Spaniards are very understanding of the difficulties immigrants face but, with a struggling economy, some Spaniards would like to see recent immigrants return to their native countries.

### IT STARTED HERE

### Locutorios

*Locutorios* are special shops that provide Internet access and phones with low call rates for immigrants to phone home. Many *Locutorios* sell special products, such as exotic fruits, and they are often the focus of a local community.

◀ Locutorios *sometimes sell particular products such as halal meat (prepared in a special way) to the Muslim community. The word* Carniceria *means 'butchers'.*

## Immigrant origins

Most immigrants in Spain come from former colonies in Latin America. They have the advantage of speaking Spanish, but many of them – especially women – do not have any qualifications and work in low-paid jobs in the tourism industry, or as domestic helpers. The second largest group comes from countries in north-west Africa, especially Morocco. Few of these immigrants speak Spanish when they arrive, and many work as unskilled labourers in the construction industry and in farming.

## Eastern European immigrants

The third largest group comes from Eastern Europe. These immigrants have helped meet Spain's need for skilled workers, especially in industries like construction. However, as the economies of the countries in Eastern Europe improve, and with Spain's economy in trouble, some workers may return home.

▶ *Spain had a booming construction industry, which attracted workers from many other countries. The recent recession has caused a slow-down in the construction industry.*

### GOING GLOBAL

Immigration has had a big impact on the pop-music culture in Spain. Top bands such as Ojos de Brujo (which means 'Wizard's Eyes') fuse Flamenco themes with other world music to create their own unique style, called 'jipjop flamenkillo'. The band has become popular in other countries, and was awarded a BBC World Music Award in 2004.

## Future challenges

Spain has had to meet the needs of its fast-growing population, and services such as schools and healthcare have to be paid for. As immigrants often work in low-paid or temporary employment this can cause problems in regions that have weak economies. In recent years the Spanish government has been refusing to renew residence permits for some recent immigrants, especially if they have become unemployed. Some of these immigrants have been put under pressure to return to their country of origin.

▲ *Although many Spanish people are tolerant of immigrants, some groups do not like the numbers of foreigners settling in their country. These people are part of a fascist group protesting against immigration.*

# Culture and lifestyles

*Spanish culture is celebrated in everyday life, not just on holidays or special occasions. There are not only famous national fiestas, such as Semana Santa (Easter week), but also each region – even every village – has its own unique Fiesta Mayor.*

## ¡Fiesta!

Dozens of different events take place during the Spanish fiestas: big events such as bulls running through the streets of Pamplona, or Valencia's Las Fallas, where huge statues – which take months to prepare – are set alight. Some events occur only in certain regions. In Catalonia, for example, *Els Castellers* make human towers or 'castles' up to 11 storeys high. Smaller towns and villages offer their own versions of traditional favourites like giants, dwarfs, dancing devils or fire-breathing dragons.

## A communal effort

All these spectacular traditions are the work of local groups, often based in communities within large cities. Some groups are small, almost family affairs, but others are huge, with hundreds of members. Many people return to their home town or village to help celebrate the fiesta, even if they moved away years ago.

▸ *Children as young as six years old train hard to reach the top of the amazing Casteller towers.*

▲ *Bull-running is a traditional event at many Spanish fiestas. People clear the way as these fearsome animals charge down the streets.*

## Catholic traditions

All fiestas are based around a serious religious celebration, usually to honour the local patron saint. Catholicism was the only religion allowed in Spain from the time the Moors left until the nineteenth century. Francisco Franco made it very difficult for non-Catholics in Spain. For example, people had to be Catholics to be allowed to work as civil servants. Since Franco's time, some Spaniards have switched to follow other Christian faiths. Large numbers of Muslims have arrived from African countries, and mosques have opened all over Spain.

### FAMOUS SPANIARD

*Penelope Cruz*
*(b. 1974)*

Spain's leading film stars such as Penelope Cruz have broken language barriers to become famous in the 'capital' of the movie world, Hollywood. Cruz was born in Madrid and began acting on television. In 2009, she was the first Spanish actress to win an Academy Award, for the film *Vicky Cristina Barcelona*.

## Sport crazy!

Football, called *futbol* in Spanish, is the most popular sport in Spain. Leading clubs such as Real Madrid and FC Barcelona attract top players from around the world and both teams excel at international football competitions. Basketball, a sport 'imported' from the USA, has become extremely popular in Spain. The Spanish basketball squad reached the final in the 2008 Beijing Olympic Games.

▼ *The Spanish basketball squad play at the highest level in Europe and internationally.*

FAMOUS SPANIARD

*Rafael Nadal (b. 1986)*

Spaniard Rafael Nadal – or Rafa, as he is known in Spain – is the world's best tennis player. He was born in Majorca and started playing tennis when he was three years old. The long-time world number one continues to win major tennis tournaments around the world.

## Popular music

Young people in Spain have been greatly influenced by aspects of popular culture from around the world. Pop groups from Britain and the USA are very popular with young Spaniards. A number of Spanish musicians and singers have also found worldwide fame, including Enrique Iglesias, who has sold over 60 million albums around the world.

## Keeping customs

Although there is a Spanish film industry, many young people enjoy American films. Some older people worry that traditional Spanish culture will be lost as young people are more exposed to the culture of English-speaking countries such as the UK and USA. However, the popularity of traditions such as fiestas keep local customs and languages alive.

## Youth culture

Children and young people are always included in all aspects of Spanish life, whether it is sport, fiestas, religion or family affairs such as Sunday lunch. They are usually allowed to stay up later than children in countries such as the UK and the USA. Spanish youngsters are extremely independent and go out on their own from their early teens. This independence often starts as young as six or seven years old, when they may attend summer camps during the school holidays, as well as children's sections of sports clubs and fiesta groups.

▲ *Groups like Calima draw music from all over the world and fuse it with Flamenco.*

## THE HOME OF...

### La Siesta

Part of the Spanish lifestyle is to take a mid-afternoon nap, called a *siesta*. In some places, shops close while people rest, and then open again later. The *siesta* makes possible the round-the-clock lifestyle that is a big feature of Spanish life.

# Economy and trade

*Membership of the EU has allowed Spain to sell its products to other countries, and has encouraged foreign companies to invest, creating jobs and generating wealth. However, like many countries, Spain has suffered in the recent global economic crisis.*

## Agriculture

Because Spain is situated in the sunny south of Europe, it is ideally suited for agriculture. Traditional crops such as olives and grapes grow well in the Spanish climate, so Spain can make olive oil and wine to sell abroad. Recently, thanks to technology such as irrigation and refrigerated transport, fruit and vegetables also grow in abundance and fetch high prices around the world, particularly in Northern Europe.

▼ *Spain's climate makes it ideal for growing crops such as grapes, and vineyards like this in Seville can be seen in many parts of the country.*

## GLOBAL LEADER

### Olive oil

Spain is the world's biggest producer of olive oil – generating 36 per cent of global production and exporting much of this to other countries. Spaniards consume nearly 14 kg of olive oil each per year. It is often used instead of butter or margarine in sandwiches.

## Industry

By the 1970s, traditional Spanish industries such as shipbuilding were facing competition from countries in the Far East, whose prices were much cheaper. To improve its own industry, Spain encouraged investment from foreign companies. Now it is a leading manufacturer of cars and electrical appliances, but although many of these products are made in Spain, the companies that make them are owned by other countries.

## Natural resources

Spain does not have a lot of natural resources. Most of its coal and iron have already been used up, so Spain has to import these materials. However, Spanish companies have been involved in finding and extracting oil and gas throughout the world. This not only supplies Spain with fuel, but also means that Spanish companies bring profits back to Spain.

▲ *Spain's important car industry is largely foreign owned. There is a risk that jobs may be lost as owners move factories abroad.*

## Real estate

Until recently, building and construction were an important part of the Spanish economy. In 2007, Spain built around 800,000 new houses – more than France, Germany and the UK put together. Since then the construction industry has collapsed, house prices have fallen and there is large scale unemployment in the industry.

## Services

Among Spain's most important service industries are finance and telecommunications. Spain is an important 'bridge' between the economies of Europe and Latin America, because Spanish banks share a common language and similar legal system. Spanish companies have also developed new technologies in these areas that can rival that of countries such as the USA.

▲ *Most building projects, especially homes, are paid for by loans or mortgages, and during the boom period families as well as companies became very much in debt.*

## GOING GLOBAL

Banco Santander is the largest bank in the Eurozone – the countries that have adopted the euro as their currency. It is part of the Santander group, Spain's largest banking corporation, which leads the banking sector in the Spanish-speaking world. As countries all over the world experienced an economic crisis in the late 2000s, the Santander group took over several big banks in countries including the UK.

## Tourism

Tourism is an important industry in Spain. World-famous sites such as Madrid's El Prado art gallery or the architecture in Barcelona attract hundreds of thousands of tourist visitors from all over the world. However, most people visit Spain to enjoy beach holidays in the hot coastal resorts. Millions of people from Northern Europe flock to Spain's Mediterranean coast to enjoy the guaranteed sunshine and relaxed lifestyle. The Spanish are enthusiastic tourists, too, and travel the world seeking new cultures and experiences.

### IT STARTED HERE

### Package holidays

Mass tourism in the sun took off in Spain after the invention of the package holiday in the 1950s. After spending many family holidays in Spain, thousands of people from Northern Europe decide to live in Spain when they retire.

▼ *Thousands of tourists visit Barcelona every year, to look at the famous architecture. Much of it – like these 'gingerbread houses' – was designed by architect Antoni Gaudí.*

*When Francisco Franco died, Spain shifted from being a dictatorship to a democracy. It adopted a new constitution, which has been very successful. Spain now has a respected role in world affairs, helped by its membership of international organizations such as the European Union, the United Nations and NATO.*

## GLOBAL LEADER

**Women in government**
Spain has a higher proportion of women cabinet ministers than any other country, with nine out of the 17 posts held by women. This means that women are the majority in the Spanish government.

## The Cortez

Franco named King Juan Carlos as his 'heir', hoping that he would continue to rule as dictator. However, Juan Carlos actually encouraged the move towards democracy, and the new constitution was adopted in 1978. Today, the Spanish parliament – called the Cortez – has two chambers, the Senate, which passes new laws, and the Congress of Deputies, which makes decisions about running the country. Many responsibilities, such as healthcare and education, are left to local governments called autonomous regions.

▼ *The* Congreso de los Diputados *(Congress of Deputies) in the Spanish parliament.*

## The role of autonomous regions

Some autonomous regions have more powers than others, and it can be difficult to achieve a balance between those who want more political freedom or even full independence, and others who want Spain to be a more united country under a single government. The Basque Country and Catalonia are the most industrialized and highly populated regions in Spain, and they attract migrants from the rest of the country as well as immigrants from abroad. The political influence of the regions is important to the Cortez, as most governments depend on co-operation between local branches of the two main political parties.

### IT'S A FACT!

There are 17 autonomous regions in Spain. Each one manages public services like healthcare and education. The regions have their own parliament and hold their own elections, as well as sending representatives to the Cortez.

▼ *Within each region there are city, or municipal councils, led by a City Mayor. These buildings in Seville house the local government offices.*

## The threat of terrorism

Catalonia and the Basque Country once owned land across the Pyrenees in France, and in the case of the Basque Country a terrorist group called ETA has used these links to hide from the police. Members of ETA want the Basque Country to be an independent state and they use terrorist methods to fight for this cause. The Spanish authorities work closely with their French counterparts to combat this threat.

## International relations

Two landmarks on Spain's move to democracy happened when it joined important international organizations – NATO in 1982 and the European Union in 1986. Some people feel that allowing the European government more control over issues such as the environment could solve some political problems over autonomy and independence. For this reason, Spaniards have been keen to support EU policies.

▲ *ETA terrorists being arrested over the border in France. ETA violence still poses a threat to Spain's stability, but membership of the EU may change the picture.*

## An Atlantic rift?

NATO is a military alliance between countries in Western Europe and the USA. General Franco allowed the Americans to build military bases in Spain long before it became a member of NATO, however, and many Spaniards feel that the USA helped Franco stay in power. Although Spain sends troops and money to NATO missions in war zones such as Afghanistan and Kosovo, it is often suspicious of US motives. In 2004, Spain withdrew its troops from the war in Iraq, as the prime minister felt that the US-led invasion was unjustified.

▲ *Crown Prince Felipe of Spain inspects Spanish troops in Afghanistan in 2008. The troops were sent there as a peacekeeping force and to help with reconstruction.*

### IT'S A FACT!

Although Spain generally has good international relationships, there are currently border disputes with Morocco (Ceuta and Melilla), Portugal (Olivenza) and the UK (Gibraltar).

# Spain in 2020

*It is likely that Spain's influence in the world will continue to grow, but it will need to recover from the serious financial crisis that beset the country in 2008. Many other issues will need to be dealt with as well, including the wealth divide between people in the north and south, and the demands by some Basque people for complete independence.*

## Regional differences

In a changing world, the Spanish people will need to unite to react to global influences such as competition for jobs and investment. However, the influence of regional governments in national affairs may make this difficult. For example, at the moment, the Catalan government is trying to gain more economic independence, and in doing so it is putting its own needs before the needs of the country as a whole. Many of the factories that were built during Spain's boom years from the mid-1960s onwards are now closing in the face of competition from Eastern Europe. Catalonia's more advanced economy may be able to meet this challenge, but other parts of Spain may not be able to compete.

◀ *Infrastructure projects, including high-speed trains and rail links – such as this in Seville – need to take the whole country into account, not just the individual regions.*

## New influences

By 2020, the governments of all the regions of Spain are likely to reflect the different ethnic groups in a way they do not at the moment. This may change the way Spain views itself and its place in the world. Even though immigration is thought to be decreasing, and some groups such as people from Eastern Europe are likely to return home as their prospects improve, the changes in society will be permanent. By 2020, a large proportion of people born in Spain will have many different ethnic origins, and all children will be raised in a country that is influenced more by the outside world than by its internal geography and history.

▶ *Festivals such as the Semana Grande celebrate the individual traditions of the Spanish regions. In the future, this pride in their unique heritage may lead some regions to demand complete independence from Spain.*

# Glossary

**autonomous** having a certain amount of political freedom. Spain's autonomous regions have some self-government, and control matters such as healthcare and education.

**colony** a country or a region that is under the political control of another country.

**constitution** a set of rules for a country, outlining the basic principles of its government.

**democracy** a political system in which the people of a country choose their leaders through elections.

**desertification** the process in which land that was once used for farming or other human activities turns into a desert.

**dictator** someone who has complete control over a country and its people.

**economy** the financial system of a country or region, including how much money is made from the production and sale of goods and services.

**Eurozone** the name given to the group of 16 countries that use the euro as their unit of currency.

**export** to transport products or materials abroad for sale or trade.

**Fascist/m** a method of government in which the ruler takes away the rights of the citizens and rules the country as a dictator.

**fossil fuels** resources from the Earth such as coal, oil and natural gas, that come from the remains of ancient plants and animals.

**hydroelectricity** electricity that is generated using the energy from running water.

**immigrant** a person who has moved to another country to live.

**import** to bring in goods or materials from another country for sale.

**Industrial Revolution** a period in the eighteenth and nineteenth centuries when machines were invented that could do work once carried out by people.

**Latin America** the parts of Central and South America where the Romance languages, originating from Latin, are spoken.

**refugee** someone who has had to flee from their own country because of war or persecution.

**renewable resources** resources that can be used for energy to make electricity that will not run out, such as wind, water and the sun.

**terrorists** people who use violence or cause fear to try and change a political system or policy.

**wetland** an area of marshy land.

# Further information

## Books

*Spain (Countries Around the World)* by Charlotte Guillain (Raintree Publishers, 2012)

*Spain (Welcome to My Country)* by G. Mesenas and K. Grinsted (Franklin Watts, 2007)

*Spain (World in Focus)* by Polly Campbell and Simon Rice (Wayland, 2006/2009)

*Spain (Discover Countries)* by Paul Harrison (Wayland, 2010)

*The European Union Today* by Simon Ponsford (Franklin Watts, 2007)

## Websites

**http://www.bbc.co.uk/schools/primaryspanish/**
Practise the Spanish language with games and animations on the BBC website.

**http://europa.eu/kids-corner/index_en.htm**
This European Union site has been set up especially for children and young people.

**http://www.travelforkids.com/Funtodo/Spain/spain.htm**
Take a journey through Spain with this fun site.

**http://www.socialstudiesforkids.com/subjects/economics.htm**
Get to grips with economics with this site where topics such as money, trade and budgets are explained.

*Every effort has been made by the publisher to ensure that these websites contain no inappropriate or offensive material. However, because of the nature of the Internet, it is impossible to guarantee that the contents of these sites will not be altered. We strongly advise that Internet access is supervised by a responsible adult.*

# Index

Numbers in **bold** indicate pictures

**A**

Afghanistan 27, **27**
Andalusia 5
architecture 5, **5**, 23, **23**
Asturias 13
Atlantic Ocean 6, 8, 13
autonomous regions 24, 25

**B**

Balearic Islands 8
Barcelona 5, **23**
basketball 18, **18**
Basque Country 6, 12, **12**, 13, 25,
  26, 28
Bilbao 6, **6**
bull-running 16, **17**

**C**

Canary Islands 4, 8, **8**, 9
Castile 4, 5
Catalonia 5, 12, 13, 16, 25, 26, 28
climate 8, 20
colonies 4, 14
constitution 24
construction 14, **14**, 22, **22**
Cordillera Cantabrica 8
Cordoba 5, **5**
Cortez 24, 25
Cruz, Penelope 17

**E**

economy 7, 13, 14, 15, 20, 21,
  22, 28
education 24, 25
Els Castellers 16, **16**
ETA 26, **26**
Europe 4, 9, 10, 14, 20, 22, 27,
  28, 29
European Union (EU) 4, 13, 20,
  24, 26
Eurozone 22

**F**

farming 14, 20
fiestas 12, **12**, 16, 17, **17**, 19
football 18
forests 9, 10
France 6, 8, 9, 13, 22, 26
Franco, Francisco 7, 13, 17, 24, 27

**G**

Galicia 6, 13
Germany 11, 13, 22
government 9, 24, **24**, 25, 26,
  28, 29

**H**

healthcare 15, 24, 25

**I**

Iglesias, Enrique 19
immigrants 12, 13, 14, 15, 25, 29
independence 25, 26, 28
Industrial Revolution 6
industry 6, 14, 21
irrigation 10, 11, 20

**J**

jobs 12, 14, 15, 20
Juan Carlos, King 24

**L**

landscape 4, 8, 9, 10
languages 4, 5, 6, 22
Latin America 7, 14, 22
Locutorios 13, **13**

**M**

Madrid 4, 7, 17, 23
Mediterranean Sea 5, 8, 10, 23
Meseta Central 8, 9, 10
Moors 5, 17
Morocco 14, 27
mosques 5, **5**, 17
mountains 4, 6, 8, **8**, 9
music 14, 19, **19**

**N**

Nadal, Rafael 18
NATO 24, 26, 27
Navarre 11
North Africa 5, 8

**O**

Ojos de Brujo 14
olive oil 20, 21

**P**

package holidays 23
population 10, 11, 12, 13, 15, 25,
  28
Pyrenees 8, 9, 13, 26

**R**

rainfall 8, 9, 10
religion 17, 19
renewable resources 11
rivers 6, 9, 10, 11

**S**

Santander 22
Siesta 19
solar power 11, **11**
Spanish Civil War 7, 13
sport 18, 19

**T**

tourism 5, 14, 23

**U**

UK 19, 22, 27
United Nations 24
USA 13, 18, 19, 22, 27

**V**

Valencia 16
voyages of discovery 4

**W**

wetlands 10, **10**
wildlife 9, 10
wine 20, **20**